STUDY GUIDE

Bill Bright

How to
REACH
YOUR
WORLD
FOR
CHRIST
*Through a New
Life Group*

T5-AMZ-453

PUBLICATIONS
A MINISTRY OF CAMPUS CRUSADE FOR CHRIST

**How to Reach Your World for Christ
Through a New Life Group: Introduction
Study Guide**

Published by
NewLife Publications
100 Sunport Lane
Orlando, FL 32809

ISBN: 1-56399-027-X

NewLife2000 is a registered service mark of Campus Crusade for Christ Inc.

Unless otherwise indicated, all Scripture references are taken from the *New International Version,* © 1973, 1978, 1984 by the International Bible Society. Published by Zondervan Bible Publishers, Grand Rapids, Michigan.

Scripture quotations designated TLB are from *The Living Bible,* © 1971 by Tyndale House Publishers, Wheaton, Illinois.

Scripture quotations designated NASB are from the *New American Standard Bible,* © 1960, 1962, 1963, 1968, 1971, 1972, 1973, 1975, 1977 by the Lockman Foundation.

For More Information, Write:
    L.I.F.E.—P.O. Box A399, Sydney South 2000, Australia
    Campus Crusade for Christ of Canada—Box 300, Vancouver, B.C., V6C 2X3, Canada
    Campus Crusade for Christ—Pearl Assurance House, 4 Temple Row, Birmingham, B2 5HG, England
    Lay Institute for Evangelism—P.O. Box 8786, Auckland 3, New Zealand
    Campus Crusade for Christ—P.O. Box 240, Raffles City Post Office, Singapore 9117
    Great Commission Movement of Nigeria—P.O. Box 500, Jos, Plateau State Nigeria, West Africa
    Campus Crusade for Christ International—100 Sunport Lane, Orlando, FL 32809, USA

Contents

A Personal Word

Jesus promised an abundant life to all who trust and obey Him. As a new Christian in 1945, I was captivated by the following statement by a famous New Testament scholar, Dr. James Stewart of Edinburgh, Scotland:

> If we could but show the world that being committed to Christ is no tame, humdrum, sheltered monotony, but the most exciting adventure the human spirit could ever know, those who have been standing outside the church and looking askance at Christ will come crowding in to pay allegiance; and we might well expect the greatest revival since Pentecost.

That is the kind of understanding and commitment to our Lord that I wanted to know and experience personally!

As I grew in my relationship to the Lord, I soon realized that the Christian life is a supernatural one. We cannot live or measure up to the high standards of our Lord and His teachings through our own human efforts. Jesus said:

> In solemn truth I tell you, anyone believing in me shall do the same miracles I have done, and even greater ones, because I am going to be with the Father. You can ask him for *anything,* using my name, and I will do it, for this will bring praise to the Father because of what I, the Son, will do for you. Yes, ask *anything,* using my name, and I will do it (John 14:12–14, TLB)!

By faith, we must draw upon the inexhaustible, supernatural resources of God to enjoy victorious, abundant, and fruitful lives. But here is the big question: How does a person learn to experience such a vital, personal relationship with our Lord?

Through training. That's why Campus Crusade for Christ was founded in 1951—to train disciples to live for the glory of God and help fulfill the Great Commission of our Lord recorded in Matthew 28:19,20.

A trained disciple is one who is assured of his salvation, who is filled with the Holy Spirit, and who knows how to deal with trials and temptations. A trained disciple also lives in the joy and wonder of the resurrection, feasting daily on God's holy, inspired Word. He communicates regularly with God in prayer and actively shares his faith. Over the years, I have become convinced that only a trained disciple can truly experience the abundant, fruitful life that Jesus promised.

Evangelism seldom produces discipleship. But biblical discipleship always results in evangelism. Although Campus Crusade is known as an evangelistic movement through which tens of millions have been introduced to Christ in all major countries of the world, our major emphasis has always been on discipleship training.

We are committed to obeying the command of Jesus to help reach the world with God's love and forgiveness through trained disciples. I have discovered that most people are afraid to share their faith in Christ. As a new Christian, I too was shy and fearful of witnessing. I remember the first time the Lord impressed me to witness to a businessman. Thinking the man would laugh at me, I resisted. Finally after many days and every argument I could think of, I yielded to the Holy Spirit's leading and found the person ready to receive Christ. Soon afterward, he left his prestigious position to attend Princeton Seminary, and has been a pastor for more than forty years.

My faith grew with that and many other experiences. Now the desire of my heart is to present Christ to everyone who will listen.

When I am alone with a person for a few minutes, I assume that I am there by divine appointment.

Shortly before midnight a few nights ago, a call came to my unlisted number. When the man on the line realized he had misdialed, he began to apologize. "I'm sorry, sir," he said, "I have a wrong number. I'm trying to call my wife. I dialed you by mistake."

"No," I quickly assured him. "It's no mistake. God has a message for you. Would you like to hear it?"

"Yes!" he replied.

I explained how much God loves him and that God has a wonderful plan for his life. We talked for a few more moments during which I learned that he and his wife were having marital difficulties. Finally, I asked, "Are you a Christian?"

"No."

"Would you like to be?"

"Oh, yes. My mother and brother are both Christians, and I have wanted to receive Christ for a long time."

"Do you know how to receive Jesus Christ as your Savior?"

"No, I don't."

I explained very simply how he could receive Christ, then suggested he pray with me—phrase by phrase—to invite Jesus into his life. After we finished praying, he expressed great gratitude and joy. Later, I rushed materials to him for assurance and spiritual growth and also arranged for personal follow-up.

After thousands of similar privileges, I am convinced of one thing: at least 50 percent of all non-believers in your "Jerusalem" and throughout the world would receive Christ if properly approached by a trained Spirit-filled believer who can communicate God's love and forgiveness revealed through our Lord Jesus Christ.

If you, too, have a deep desire to introduce others to Jesus, I encourage you to receive training in how to share your faith. Begin every day with a prayer like this:

> Lord, lead me to someone today whose heart You have prepared to receive the joyful news of our loving Savior. Enable me to be Your messenger to show others how to find forgiveness of sin and the gift of eternal life. Amen.

As you rise from your knees and go out into your world to study or work, the Holy Spirit will honor that simple, earnest prayer and guide you to those whom He has prepared for your witness. As you meet people in the course of your day, ask the Lord, "Is it he? Is it she? Where is the person You want me to introduce to You?"

Always carry a *Four Spiritual Laws* booklet or a similar presentation so that when the "divine appointment" occurs and you recognize the opportunity, you can aggressively share your faith. Whether or not they receive Christ, leave them with the *Gospel of John*, the *Man Without Equal* book, the *Four Spiritual Laws,* or something similar to read.

This *New Life Group* study is designed to train you to grow as a disciple to live a godly life and share your faith in Christ as a way of life. All you need is a desire to apply the biblical principles in these lessons to your life and a commitment to help others grow in Christ.

Being part of a *New Life Group* will be one of the most exciting adventures of your lifetime. God will richly bless you for your obedience to His Word, and you will experience the reality of our Lord's promise to all who love and obey Him: "I will reveal myself to you" (John 14:21).

Changing Your World

Do you have a deep desire to see others come to know Jesus personally like you do? Are you unsure about how to challenge believers to apply biblical principles to their lives? Let me share an exciting way to reach your world for Christ through a *New Life Group*.

I am constantly amazed at the way God uses people like you and me to change lives. Let me tell you about a village in Thailand. The town had only five Christians. It had been that way for more than twenty-five years. Then one day, a person trained to show the "JESUS" Film came to that village and asked these Christians if they would hold *New Life Groups* in their homes for people who wanted to know more about Jesus after the film was shown. Three of them agreed to open their homes to train new believers.

God performed miracles through these small groups. During the training session, 227 people received Christ. These trainees began reaching out to the five villages nearby, soon increasing the total of new Christians to 444. These believers were then organized into *New Life Groups* as well.

I have seen God work in similar ways all over the world. Whether you live in a small village, a bustling city, or a major metropolis in any country or on any continent, you can learn how to introduce your friends, neighbors, and relatives to Jesus Christ. God can use you to make a difference in their lives. Then you can help train them to win and disciple others according to 2 Timothy 2:2, "The things you have heard me say in the presence of many witnesses entrust to reliable men who will also be qualified to teach others."

God has given clear guidelines on how you can accomplish this. They are found in the words "commandment" and "commission."

Christ's "Great Commandment" is recorded in Matthew 22:37–40:

> "Love the Lord your God with all your heart and with all your soul and with all your mind." This is the first and greatest commandment. And the second is like it: "Love your neighbor as yourself." All the Law and the Prophets hang on these two commandments.

Apart from love, nothing has ever been accomplished for the glory of God or the good of mankind. Love is the spiritual glue that enables society to function. As Christians, you and I have the power and the responsibility to love others with God's love. We can love by faith on the basis of God's *command* to love and His *promise* recorded in 1 John 5:14,15:

> If we ask anything according to his will, he hears us. And if we know that he hears us—whatever we ask—we know that we have what we asked of him.

Being a part of a *New Life Group* will enable you to be part of history's most glorious task—helping to fulfill our Lord's Great Commission. Jesus said:

> Go and make disciples of all nations, baptizing them in the name of the Father and of the Son and of the Holy Spirit, and teaching them to obey everything I have commanded you (Matthew 28:19,20).

By early 1993, more than 200,000 *New Life Groups* had already been established throughout the world. By joining a *New Life Group,* you will become part of what could well be the single largest and most effective strategy to help fulfill the Great Commission since our Lord gave it almost 2,000 years ago. This strategy is called *NewLife2000®*. Let me explain...

NewLife2000

NewLife2000 is the overall, worldwide master strategy of Campus Crusade for Christ International to help fulfill the Great Commission. The strategy encompasses each of the many Campus Crusade ministries in the United States and overseas. Millions of

Christians in thousands of churches of all major denominations and hundreds of mission groups from many Christian denominations are participating in this global effort. The strategy calls for presenting the gospel (the good news that Jesus brings us new life) through 10,000 "JESUS" Film teams and other effective evangelistic tools. *NewLife2000* has divided the world into 5,000 MPTAs (Million-Population Target Areas). Working in cooperation with millions of Christians in thousands of churches and hundreds of mission groups, the goal is to:

- Expose more than six billion people to the gospel

- Introduce more than one billion people to Christ using the "JESUS" Film, the *Four Spiritual Laws, A Man Without Equal* video, and other evangelistic tools

- Help participating denominations plant one million new churches

- Launch ministries on 8,000 college campuses in strategic metropolitan areas worldwide

- Help establish more than 20 million *New Life Groups*

By January 1993, more than one-and-a-half billion people had heard the gospel through this ministry. The "JESUS" Film alone had been viewed by more than 500 million people in 250 languages in 194 countries, representing 98 percent of the world's population. Tens of millions of people had invited Christ into their lives as Savior and Lord.

To help these new Christians grow in Christ, *Great Commission Training Centers, New Life Training Centers,* and *New Life Groups* are being established all over the world.

A *Great Commission Training Center* provides a nine-month course that teaches people to grow and mature in their Christian faith.

A *New Life Training Center* provides students with approximately one hundred hours of instruction in evangelism and discipleship. About half of that time is spent in field application.

New Life Groups meet weekly for fellowship, Bible study, prayer, and training in how to live a holy life and how to share their faith through the power of the Holy Spirit. The members in these groups are encouraged to continue their training at the nearest *New Life Training Center.*

As a member of a *New Life Group,* you can be part of this strategy. You can become a dynamic force for God and an important part of His plan by touching the lives of your friends, neighbors, or relatives for Christ. Let me explain how a *New Life Group* works.

A *New Life Group* is a small gathering of Christian believers who meet weekly for fellowship, Bible study, prayer, and training. Through small New-Testament-like meetings, you will:

- Explore the basics of the Christian faith
- Be sure you are a Christian
- Begin growing spiritually with God's help
- Learn how to share your faith in Christ with others

As you begin studying these lessons, God will open your mind and heart to the truths presented here. I am confident that your learning will result in spiritual growth and will be one of the most rewarding experiences of your life.

Who Is Jesus?

Who Is God?

God has a personality with definite characteristics. Look up these verses and write down the qualities you find.

1. Psalm 90:2

2. Hebrews 1:12

3. Psalm 147:5

4. Romans 11:33

5. 1 Samuel 2:2

6. Job 34:10–12

7. 1 John 4:8

The Uniqueness of Jesus

Jesus lived the most extraordinary life in the history of mankind. Look up these verses and write down how Jesus is like no one else in the areas listed:

1. The Old Testament prophecies of His coming: Psalm 16:10; Isaiah 52:13–15; Micah 5:2; Zechariah 9:9

2. His birth: Matthew 1:18–2:12; Luke 1:26–2:20

3. His childhood: Luke 2:21–52

4. His teachings: Matthew 5–7; Mark 4; Luke 8:4–18

5. His miracles: Matthew 8:14–34; Mark 8:1–30; Luke 8:22–56; John 5:31–39

6. His death and resurrection: Matthew 20:17–19; Matthew 28:1–10; Mark 14–16; Luke 22–24; John 18–21

The Claims of Jesus

Jesus made many claims about Himself. Use this chart to explore these claims. How do they affect your life?

Jesus said He was:	How it affects my life	Scripture reference
The Judge of the world		Matthew 7:21–23
The fulfillment of Scripture		Luke 24:44
The "I am"		John 8:54–59; 18:5,6
Divine		Matthew 4:7; 12:6–8; Mark 14:61–64
The Light of the World		John 8:12; 9:5

Jesus said He was:	How it affects my life	Scripture reference
Sinless and eternal		John 8:46,58; 14:30; 17:5
Able to save the lost		Luke 19:10; John 10:9; 11:25
Able to forgive sins		Mark 2:5; Luke 7:48–50

You can experience the exciting adventure of living for Jesus. He offers:

- Freedom from anxiety (Matthew 6:25–34)
- Inner peace (John 16:33)
- Answers to your prayers (1 John 5:14,15)

Action Point: Write down any situations this week in which these verses help you live above your circumstances and how you have had victory over trials and temptations.

LESSON 2

How You Can Be Sure You Are a Christian

The New Birth

Receiving Jesus Christ as Savior means experiencing a new, spiritual birth. Read John 3:1–8 and write a description of this new birth.

Our relationship with Christ involves three areas of commitment: intellect, emotions, and will. Which area creates the most problems for you?

Intellectual Commitment

Christianity is not a "blind" leap of faith, but a personal relationship with God through Jesus Christ. Read John 10:30–33 and 14:6–9. How does Jesus' claim to be one with the Father ensure His ability to forgive sins?

According to Romans 1:3,4, what is the ultimate proof of Christ's claim to be God?

How does this affect your life (verses 5,6,16,17)?

Emotional Commitment

Seeking an emotional experience contradicts Hebrews 11:6. Faith is another word for trust. This trust must be placed in God and His Word rather than in what we feel. In what situations do you tend to trust in feelings rather than in God's Word?

This diagram shows how we should let faith control our lives.

How can you let your faith control these situations? List specific ways you plan to do this.

Commitment of the Will

A commitment to Christ involves an act of the will. Although both mind and feelings are valid, you are not a Christian until, as an act of your will, you make a decision to receive Christ as your Savior and Lord.

Have you taken this step?

When?

The Basis of Your Relationship with Christ

- What is the message of the gospel? (1 Corinthians 15:1–4)

- Why did Christ have to die? (1 Corinthians 15:3; Hebrews 9:22)

- What happens when a person responds to the gospel and receives Christ into his life? (John 1:12)

Our Confidence in Christ

If our relationship with God were dependent on our own good works, we could never have assurance of salvation. Read Ephesians 2:8,9 and answer these questions:

- What is grace?

- In what are we to have faith? (See Galatians 3:22,26.)

- Why is boasting not acceptable?

Rewrite Ephesians 2:8,9 and Galatians 3:22–26 in words you would use to explain the verses to a friend.

God's Promises to All Christians

What do these verses promise you as a result of your decision to trust in Christ?

- Revelation 3:20

- 1 John 5:11–13

- John 10:27–29

- John 5:24

Which promise is most meaningful to you?

Why?

How can you apply these verses to strengthen your faith?

Action Point: This coming week, explain to a friend why you are sure you are a Christian.

How You Can Experience God's Love and Forgiveness

Three Types of People

The Bible describes three types of people in 1 Corinthians, chapters 2 and 3. Underline the characteristics of each. Determine which type of life you are living.

- The *natural person* (1 Corinthians 2:14) is not a Christian. He depends on his own resources and lives in his own strength. Spiritually, he is dead to God—separated from God by sin.

Self-Directed Life
S – Self is on the throne
† – Christ is outside the life
● – Interests are directed by
  self, often resulting in
  discord and frustration

- The *spiritual person* (1 Corinthians 2:15,16) is a Christian who is controlled and empowered by the Holy Spirit. He draws upon the unlimited resources of God's love and power and lives in the strength of the living Christ. He is alive to God because the Son of God is living in and through him. He brings glory to God because of his fruitful life and witness.

Christ-Directed Life

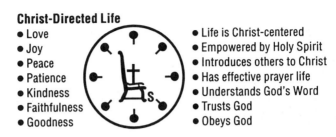

- Love
- Joy
- Peace
- Patience
- Kindness
- Faithfulness
- Goodness

- Life is Christ-centered
- Empowered by Holy Spirit
- Introduces others to Christ
- Has effective prayer life
- Understands God's Word
- Trusts God
- Obeys God

■ The *worldly person* (1 Corinthians 3:1–3) is a believer trying to live the Christian life in his own strength. He is a defeated, fruitless Christian, who depends on his own abilities instead of drawing upon the inexhaustible resources of the Holy Spirit. He lives in frustration and slavery to sin (Romans 7:14–20).

Self-Directed Life

- Legalistic attitude
- Impure thoughts
- Jealousy
- Guilt
- Worry
- Discouragement
- Critical spirit
- Frustration
- Aimlessness
- Fear

- Ignorance of his spiritual heritage
- Unbelief
- Disobedience
- Loss of love for God and for others
- Poor prayer life
- No desire for Bible study

I am living the life of the _____ person.

Spiritual Breathing

A spiritual man lives by faith in God. Faith is trusting that God will do what He says He will do. When we place our faith in God and His Word, we can experience His love and power.

How can we get off the emotional, roller-coaster existence of a worldly life? By practicing "Spiritual Breathing," which is *exhaling* the impure (confessing our sins) and *inhaling* the pure (appropriating the power of the Holy Spirit as an act of our will by faith), 1 John 1:9; Ephesians 5:18.

Handling Guilt

When you feel guilty, compare your feelings to the criteria in this checklist, then circle the correct responses below. Follow the directions you have circled.

Checklist for Finding the Source of Guilt
When the Holy Spirit convicts me of sin: ■ He will point out a specific sin, and ■ God will forgive the sin and restore my fellowship with Him as soon as I confess it. The guilt is immediately lifted. I am feeling false guilt if: ■ My feelings of guilt are vague and unspecific, or ■ I am feeling guilty over a sin that I previously and sincerely confessed to God.
Circle one: My feelings of guilt are (real) (false) so I will (exhale—confess it to God) (thank God that His forgiveness is immediate and complete).

Action Point: To *exhale,* follow these steps:

1. Ask the Lord to reveal any unconfessed sins. Write them on a piece of paper.

2. Confess these sins (agree with God that they are wrong).

3. Write 1 John 1:9 across the top. Destroy the list.

4. Make plans for restitution where you have wronged someone.

LESSON 4

How You Can Be Filled With the Holy Spirit

Answer the following questions from the verses given.

Who Is the Holy Spirit?

- Acts 5:3,4

- 1 Thessalonians 5:19; Ephesians 4:30

  How do you know He is a person and not a force or impersonal power? 1 Corinthians 2:11; 12:11; Romans 15:30

- Matthew 28:19; 2 Corinthians 13:14

Why Did the Holy Spirit Come?

- John 16:7,8,13,14

- John 7:37–39

- Acts 1:8

- Romans 8:26

- Ephesians 1:13,14

What Does It Mean to Be Filled With the Spirit?

To be filled with the Spirit is to be filled with Jesus Christ, the risen Son of God, and to abide in Him. Since God is one shown through three persons, the Holy Spirit is the essence of Jesus. *Filled* means to be directed, controlled, and empowered by the Holy Spirit. When I am filled with the Spirit, Christ's Spirit will dwell in my body and live His resurrection life in and through me.

1. What is the difference between being filled with wine and being filled with the Spirit?

2. Why is a person different when he is filled with either one of these agents?

The Fruits of the Spirit

Read John 15:1–5,8.

1. What comparison can you draw between the relationship of a vine to a branch and of Christ to a Christian?

2. What does "fruit" mean in verse 8?

How to Be Filled With the Holy Spirit

Although all Christians are indwelt by the Spirit, not all are filled with the Spirit. Most Christians are not filled with the Spirit because of:

- Lack of knowledge

- Unbelief

What is keeping you from being filled with the Spirit?

Action Point: To be filled with the Spirit, practice Spiritual Breathing.

Exhale:

- Ask the Holy Spirit to show you any unconfessed sin.

- Confess your sin and claim the promise of 1 John 1:9.

- Make restitution if necessary.

Inhale:

- Claim the filling of the Holy Spirit by faith on the basis of God's *command* and God's *promise* (Ephesians 5:18, 1 John 5:14,15).

Here is a prayer you can use:

Dear Father, I need You. I acknowledge that I have been in control of my own life and have sinned against You. I thank You for forgiving my sins through Christ's death on the cross for me. I now invite Christ to take control of my life. Fill me with the Holy Spirit as You commanded me to be filled. You promised in Your Word that You would fill me if I ask in faith. As an expression of my faith, I now thank You for filling me with Your Holy Spirit and for taking control of my life. Amen.

How You Can Walk In the Spirit

LESSON 5

As best you can, chart your spiritual well-being for the past few weeks, showing any "highs" or "lows" or steady progress you have made in applying Spiritual Breathing.

My Christian Walk

Perfect Success ————————————————————

Dismal Failure ————————————————————

Barriers to Walking in the Spirit

1. Barrier of Unconfessed Sin

Sin will not affect our relationship with God; that is permanent. Sin, however, will break our fellowship with God. Match the statements on the left with the answers on the right.

A. Our relationship with God is:

B. Our fellowship with God is:

1. Restored by confessing sin
2. Maintained by God
3. Capable of being broken
4. Maintained in part by us
5. Eternally secure
6. Begun at salvation

Practicing Spiritual Breathing is a means to deal with uncon-fessed sin. List the steps to Spiritual Breathing.

1.

2.

3.

2. *Barrier of Self Effort*
Read Romans 7:15–20.

1. What is the source of Paul's struggle in this passage?

2. How did that make him feel?

3. When have you experienced similar frustration?

3. *Barrier of Circumstances*
Many Christians allow circumstances to sway their faith. But we are to live by faith and believe in the trustworthiness of God's Word. The train diagram illustrates the relationship between:

- Fact (God and His Word)
- Faith (our trust in God and His Word)
- Feeling (the result of our faith and obedience)

How can you be sure you are walking by faith rather than feelings?

Dealing With Barriers

List three areas of your life—such as dating, finances, or family concerns—and describe how placing your faith in God's Word would affect each circumstance.

1.

2.

3.

Action Point: Whenever a circumstance or temptation threatens to become a barrier between you and God this week, review this chart and reaffirm your commitment to walk in the Spirit.

Walking in the Spirit	Trusts in God and His Word	Experiences forgiveness through confession	Believes God in order to be filled with His Spirit	God causes growth and fruitfulness
Walking in Self Effort	Trusts in self	Sin brings guilt or rationalization	Increased effort to live by God's standards	Frustration and defeat

LESSON 6

How You Can Grow As a Christian

Read 2 Peter 3:18. What is the result of spiritual growth?

Principle One: We Must Read the Bible

1. Jesus said, "Man shall not live by bread alone." How did He say that we should live and be nourished? (Matthew 4:4)

2. The Bible is often referred to as "the Word of God" because it contains God's words to us. Why is reading God's Word so important? (2 Timothy 3:16,17)

3. What will result in your life when you read God's Word? (Psalm 119:11,105)

Principle Two: We Must Pray

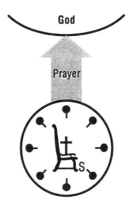

When praying, remember these things:

1. Pray about everything. (Philippians 4:6,7)

   What is the result if we talk to God about everything?

2. Pray specifically. (John 14:14, 16:24)

   Why do you think it is important to pray specifically?

   What will be two results of praying specifically?

3. Pray continually. (1 Thessalonians 5:17)

   What does the Bible mean when it says to pray continually?

Principle Three: We Must Fellowship With Other Christians

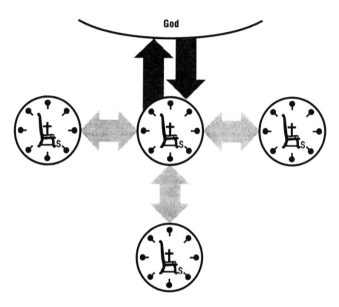

1. As God's children, what should we not neglect? (Hebrews 10:24,25)

   Why?

2. What are the basic functions of a local church? (Colossians 1:25–28; 2 Timothy 4:2)

3. The new believers in the early church continued steadfastly in what four things? (Acts 2:41,42)

   a.

   b.

   c.

   d.

4. If we spend 90 percent of our time with non-Christians and 10 percent with Christians, which group will have the greater influence on our lives?

   Why?

Principle Four: We Must Witness for Christ

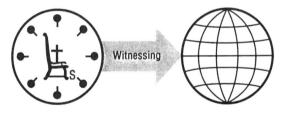

1. What is the greatest thing that has ever happened to you?

2. What, then, is the greatest thing that you can do for another person?

3. In Romans 1:14–16, Paul tells us his own attitude about sharing the good news of Jesus Christ with others. Using

his three "I's" as the keys to the passage, describe his attitude in your own words.

4. What was Jesus' promise in Acts 1:8?

Write down the names of several people with whom you plan to share your faith in Christ during the next week.

_____ _____

_____ _____

Principle Five: We Must Obey God

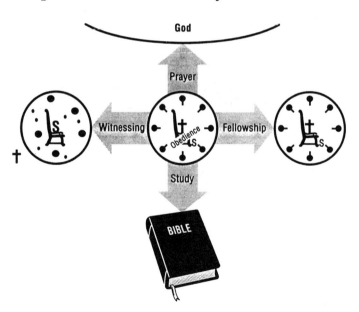

1. How can you prove that you love the Lord? (John 14:21)

2. What will be the result of keeping Christ's commandments? (John 15:10)

   What does that mean to you?

3. Where do we get the power to obey God? (Philippians 2:13)

4. In light of Christ's illustration in Luke 6:46–49, why would you say that obedience to Christ is imperative for your life?

Fill out the first chart to plan your quiet time for the next week. Use the second chart during your quiet time.

My Quiet Time with God							
Day	Sun.	Mon.	Tue.	Wed.	Thur.	Fri.	Sat.
Date							
Time							
Prayer requests							
Scripture passage							

Specific Prayers Made	Date of Prayer	Date of Answer
1.		
2.		
3.		
4.		
5.		
6.		

Have You Heard
of the
Four Spiritual Laws?

Just as there are physical laws that govern the physical universe, so are there spiritual laws that govern your relationship with God.

LAW ONE

GOD **LOVES** YOU AND HAS A WONDERFUL **PLAN** FOR YOUR LIFE.

God's Love
"God so loved the world that He gave His only begotten Son, that whoever believes in Him should not perish, but have eternal life" (John 3:16).

God's Plan
[Christ speaking] "I came that they might have life, and might have it abundantly" [that it might be full and meaningful] (John 10:10).

Why is it that most people are not experiencing the abundant life?

Because...

LAW TWO

MAN IS **SINFUL** AND **SEPARATED** FROM GOD. THUS HE CANNOT KNOW AND EXPERIENCE GOD'S LOVE AND PLAN FOR HIS LIFE.

Man Is Sinful
"All have sinned and fall short of the glory of God" (Romans 3:23).

Man was created to have fellowship with God; but, because of his own stubborn self-will, he chose to go his own independent way and fellowship with God was broken. This self-will, characterized by an attitude of active rebellion or passive indifference, is an evidence of what the Bible calls sin.

Man Is Separated
"The wages of sin is death" [spiritual separation from God] (Romans 6:23).

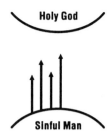

This diagram illustrates that God is holy and man is sinful. A great chasm separates the two. The arrows illustrate that man is continually trying to reach God and the abundant life through his own efforts: good life, ethics, philosophy, and more.

The Third Law gives us the only answer to this dilemma...

LAW THREE

JESUS CHRIST IS GOD'S **ONLY** PROVISION FOR MAN'S SIN. THROUGH HIM YOU CAN KNOW AND EXPERIENCE GOD'S LOVE AND PLAN FOR YOUR LIFE.

He Died In Our Place
"God demonstrates His own love toward us, in that while we were yet sinners, Christ died for us" (Romans 5:8).

He Rose from the Dead
"Christ died for our sins... He was buried... He was raised on the third day, according to the Scriptures... He appeared to Peter, then to the twelve. After that He appeared to more than five hundred..." (1 Corinthians 15:3–6).

He Is the Only Way to God
"Jesus said to him, 'I am the way, and the truth, and the life; no one comes to the Father but through Me'" (John 14:6).

This diagram illustrates that God has bridged the chasm that separates us from Him by sending His Son, Jesus Christ, to die on the cross in our place to pay the penalty for our sins.

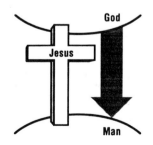

It is not enough to know these three laws...

LAW FOUR

WE MUST INDIVIDUALLY **RECEIVE** JESUS CHRIST AS SAVIOR AND LORD; THEN WE CAN KNOW AND EXPERIENCE GOD'S LOVE AND PLAN FOR OUR LIVES.

We Must Receive Christ

"As many as received Him, to them He gave the right to become children of God, even to those who believe in His name" (John 1:12).

We Receive Christ Through Faith

"By grace you have been saved through faith; and that not of yourselves, it is the gift of God; not as a result of works that no one should boast" (Ephesians 2:8,9).

When We Receive Christ, We Experience a New Birth

(Read John 3:1–8.)

We Receive Christ Through Personal Invitation

[Christ speaking] "Behold, I stand at the door and knock; if any one hears My voice and opens the door, I will come in to him" (Revelation 3:20).

Receiving Christ involves turning to God from self (repentance) and trusting Christ to come into our lives to forgive our sins and to make us what He wants us to be. Just to agree intellectually that Jesus Christ is the Son of God and that He died on the cross for our sins is not enough. Nor is it enough to have an emotional experience. We receive Jesus Christ by faith, as an act of the will.

These two circles represent two kinds of lives:

Self-Directed Life
S – Self is on the throne
† – Christ is outside the life
● – Interests are directed by self, often resulting in discord and frustration

Christ-Directed Life
† – Christ is in the life and on the throne
S – Self is yielding to Christ
● – Interests are directed by Christ, resulting in harmony with God's plan

Which circle best represents your life?

Which circle would you like to have represent your life?

The following explains how you can receive Christ:

YOU CAN RECEIVE CHRIST RIGHT NOW BY FAITH THROUGH PRAYER

(Prayer is talking with God)

God knows your heart and is not so concerned with your words as He is with the attitude of your heart. The following is a suggested prayer:

> *Lord Jesus, I need You. Thank You for dying on the cross for my sins. I open the door of my life and receive You as my Savior and Lord. Thank You for forgiving my sins and giving me eternal life. Take control of the throne of my life. Make me the kind of person You want me to be.*

Does this prayer express the desire of your heart?

If it does, pray this prayer right now, and Christ will come into your life, as He promised.

How to Know That Christ Is in Your Life

Did you receive Christ into your life? According to His promise in Revelation 3:20, where is Christ right now in relation to you?

Christ said that He would come into your life. Would He mislead you? On what authority do you know that God has answered your prayer? (The trustworthiness of God Himself and His Word.)

The Bible Promises Eternal Life to All Who Receive Christ

"The witness is this, that God has given us eternal life, and this life is in His Son. He who has the Son has the life; he who does not have the Son of God does not have the life. These things I have written to you who believe in the name of the Son of God, in order that you may know that you have eternal life" (1 John 5:11–13).

Thank God often that Christ is in your life and that He will never leave you (Hebrews 13:5). You can know on the basis of His promise that the living Christ indwells you and that you have eternal life from the very moment you invite Him in. He will not deceive you.

Note: All Scripture references are from the *New American Standard Bible*.

Resources to Help You Study the Lessons

Title	Unit Price	Qty.	Total
How to Reach Your World for Christ			

How to Reach Your World for Christ
Leader's Kit, includes:
    5 Introductory Study Guides
    1 A Man Without Equal video
  50 Four Spiritual Laws booklets
  50 Spirit-Filled Life booklets
Retail value: $34.00
	19.99		

How to Reach Your World for Christ Full curriculum. Complete Leader's Guide for: Introduction, Sharing Your New Life, and Multiplying Your New Life Bible studies.	10.99		

How to Reach Your World for Christ: Introduction
Teaches new believers the biblical truth about salvation, steps to growing, understanding God's love, experiencing God's forgiveness, and being filled with the Holy Spirit.
    Leader's Guide
    Study Guide
	
	5.99
	4.99		

How to Reach Your World for Christ: Sharing Your New Life Study Guide for a ten-week Bible study that builds on the introductory six-week Bible study. Students learn how to share their faith, pray effectively, and develop a relationship with Christ.	4.99		
How to Reach Your World for Christ: Multiplying Your New Life Study Guide for the second ten-week Bible study. Students will discover how to find God's will for their lives, follow-up new believers, and be challenged to begin their own New Life Group.	4.99		
Transferable Concepts			
Transferable Concepts (Set of 10 books) Exciting tools to help you experience and share the abundant Christian life. See Resource section in each lesson for books you may want to use in your study. Choose from individual books below:	19.50		

Title	Unit Price	Qty.	Total
How You Can Be Sure You Are a Christian *Resource for Lesson 2*	1.99		
How You Can Experience God's Love and Forgiveness *Resource for Lesson 3*	1.99		
How You Can Be Filled With the Spirit *Resource for Lesson 4*	1.99		
How You Can Walk in the Spirit *Resource for Lesson 5*	1.99		
How You Can Be a Fruitful Witness *Resource for Lesson 6*	1.99		
How You Can Introduce Others to Christ *Resource for Lesson 6*	1.99		
How You Can Help Fulfill the Great Commission	1.99		
How You Can Love By Faith	1.99		
How You Can Pray With Confidence *Resource for Lesson 6*	1.99		
How You Can Experience the Adventure of Giving	1.99		
Ten Basic Steps for Christian Maturity			
Ten Basic Steps A comprehensive curriculum for the Christian who wants to master the basics of Christian growth. Used by hundreds of thousands worldwide.			
The Ten Basic Steps Leader's Guide Contains Bible study outlines for teaching the complete series.	14.99		
The Handbook for Christian Maturity Combines the entire series of the *Ten Basic Steps* in one volume. A handy resource for private Bible study, an excellent book to help nurture spiritual growth and maturity.	12.99		
Introduction: The Uniqueness of Jesus	4.99		
Step 1: The Christian Adventure	4.99		

Title	Unit Price	Qty.	Total
Step 2: The Christian and the Abundant Life	4.99		
Step 3: The Christian and the Holy Spirit	4.99		
Step 4: The Christian and Prayer	4.99		
Step 5: The Christian and the Bible	4.99		
Step 6: The Christian and Obedience	4.99		
Step 7: The Christian and Witnessing	4.99		
Step 8: The Christian and Giving	4.99		
Step 9: Exploring the Old Testament	4.99		
Step 10: Exploring the New Testament	4.99		
Other Resources Available			
A Man Without Equal (video) Intriguing 30-minute video explores the uniqueness of Jesus through dramatic recreations and breathtaking portraits from the great Masters. An effective evangelism tool. This video can be used to help start your New Life Group.	14.99		
A Man Without Equal (book) A fresh look at the unique birth, teachings, death, and resurrection of Jesus and how He continues to change the way we live and think. Good as an evangelistic tool. *Resource for Lesson 1*	4.99		
Jesus: The Man Who Changed the World (video) The vast panorama of history shows the unmistakable influence of Jesus Christ on people and nations. This 30-minute video describes His impact on civilization and challenges Christians to let Him change their life and their world.	14.99		
Four Spiritual Laws booklet (pkg. of 50) One of the most effective evangelistic tools ever developed. An easy-to-use way of sharing your faith with others.	7.99		
Spirit-Filled Life booklet (pkg. of 25) Discover the reality of the Spirit-filled life and how to live in moment-by-moment dependence on Him.	5.99		

Title	Unit Price	Qty.	Total
Life Without Equal A presentation of the length and breadth of the Christian's freedom in Jesus Christ and how believers can release Christ's resurrection power for life and ministry. Good for unbelievers or Christians who want to grow in their Christian life. *Resource for Lesson 6*	4.99		
Witnessing Without Fear A step-by-step guide to sharing your faith with confidence. Ideal for both individual and group study; a Gold Medallion winner.	8.99		
The Holy Spirit: The Key to Supernatural Living This book helps you enter into the Spirit-filled life and shares how you can experience a life of supernatural power and victory.	6.99		
Keys to Dynamic Living (3×5 card; pkg. of 5) Experience a joyful, fruitful, Spirit-filled life and deal with temptation through "spiritual listening" and "spiritual breathing." Small enough to tuck into your pocket, purse, or Bible.	2.50		

BILLING INFORMATION

☐ Enclosed is my check payable to *Campus Crusade for Christ*

☐ Bill my MasterCard, VISA, or Discover card (circle one)

Card Number_____

Expiration Date_____ / _____

Signature_____

DELIVERY ADDRESS

Name_____

Address_____

City_____

State _____ Zip _____

Phone (_____) _____

Subtotal all items _____

Less multiple purchase discount (see chart below) _____

CA shipments add 7.75% sales tax _____

Shipping & handling add 10% or $3.00, whichever is greater _____

Total Amount Due $ _____

MULTIPLE PURCHASE DISCOUNTS
5-9 items: 10% off • 10-14 items: 15% off
15 or more items: 20% off

MAIL TO:

NewLife Publications
Campus Crusade for Christ
Arrowhead Springs 31-00
San Bernardino, CA 92414

BILL BRIGHT is founder and president of Campus Crusade for Christ International. Serving in 152 major countries representing 98 percent of the world's population, he and his dedicated associates of more than 40,000 full-time staff and trained volunteers have introduced tens of millions of people to Jesus Christ, discipling millions to live Spirit-filled, fruitful lives of purpose and power for the glory of God.

Dr. Bright did graduate study at Princeton and Fuller Theological seminaries from 1946 to 1951. The recipient of many national and international awards, including five honorary doctorates, he is the author of numerous books and publications committed to helping fulfill the Great Commission. His special focus is New Life 2000, an international effort to help reach more than six billion people with the gospel of our Lord Jesus Christ and help fulfill the Great Commission by the year 2000.

Notes

Notes

Notes